BYZANTINE EMPIRE

A History From Beginning to End

Copyright © 2017 by Hourly History.

All rights reserved.

Table of Contents

Introduction
A Divided Empire
The Fall of the West
Rising to Glory
An Age of War
The Destruction of Icons
The House of Macedon
The Comnenian Revival
The Final Decline
Conclusion

Introduction

The history of the medieval era brings to mind the feudal system with its handful of nobles constantly fighting for territory and the competing forces of various kingdoms and the all-powerful church. But these are pictures of Western Europe. In the east, a different picture emerged—one often neglected in our image of the Middle Ages. In the Byzantine Empire, centered around the city of Constantinople (modern Istanbul) and the realm of Asia Minor, a powerful civilization carried the torch of classical civilization for nearly a millennium after the fall of Rome. In Byzantium, the emperor retained ultimate power, allowing for a stable central government. The church and the government largely worked together rather than against one another. Byzantium brought great works of art and architecture into being and preserved Greek literature and knowledge for the ages. Despite a series of formidable foes, rebellions and natural disasters, and the shifting forces of Europe and the east, Byzantium developed a culture like no other—one which continues to impact the world today.

The story of the Byzantine Empire is, of necessity, often a story of the men and women who shaped the empire: the emperors who took the throne peacefully or through bloodshed; the powerful women, wives and mothers, who influenced emperors or held power in their own right; the generals who commanded armies to stem the tide of invasions. While these figures are preserved for us in the records of history, it is left for us to imagine the world they shaped. Byzantium was an agricultural society, a hub of world trade, and the center of the Eastern Church. Merchants, sailors, monks and nuns, farmers, artisans, and tradespeople populated its lands. In this book, you'll discover the story of an often-forgotten piece of the past: the intrigues, wars, leaders, political gambles, religious controversies, and cultural developments that shaped Byzantium into a major force in the medieval world.

Chapter One

A Divided Empire

"[Constantine] saw with his own eyes the trophy of a cross of light in the heavens, above the sun, and bearing the inscription, 'Conquer by this.'"

—Eusebius

In 330 CE, the date assigned by historians as the beginning of the Byzantine Empire, the nobles, merchants, soldiers, and sailors pushing their way through the busy streets of Byzantium would not have seen themselves as standing on the edge of a new empire. Instead, they still called themselves *Rhomaioi*—Romans, the people of the Roman Empire. The terms "Byzantines" and the "Byzantine Empire" would not come into use until the sixteenth century. Until then, the Byzantine Empire was simply the Eastern Roman Empire, the extension of the ancient imperium.

The splitting of the Roman Empire into east and west began almost 50 years before the assigned date marking the start of the Byzantine Empire. In 284, Diocletian rose to power in the east. Within a year, he also took control of the west. He realized that the enormous size of the empire made it difficult to rule, especially at a time of instability. His solution was innovative—he took the position of

Augustus, senior emperor, and assigned his friend Maximian the title of Caesar, junior emperor. Before long, Diocletian raised Maximian to Augustus as well and put him in charge of the western part of the empire. Both emperors took Caesars to help them rule the still-expansive halves of the empire. Together, the four rulers formed a tetrarchy; their ability to work together brought stability to the weakening empire. They successfully put down revolts and repelled invaders. In 305, Diocletian and Maximian stepped down from power voluntarily. They aimed to peacefully pass on the empire to their Caesars, who would choose new junior emperors to continue the tetrarchy.

Though Diocletian left systems for taxation and bureaucracy in place that would help to keep the Eastern Roman Empire stable for centuries, his plan to pass on the tetrarchy did not work out the way he intended. In the west, the succession was complicated by the death of the Augustus, Constantius, and his army's subsequent announcement that Constantius' son Constantine would be the new Augustus. The eastern Augustus, Galerius, compromised and agreed for Constantine to become the west's Caesar instead. The orderly progression was disrupted, and before long Maximian's son Maxentius promoted himself to emperor, conquering the territory of the current western Augustus. Now all four members of the tetrarchy claimed the title of Augustus, and the once cooperative relationships between the emperors disintegrated.

Constantine, allying himself with one of the eastern emperors, marched against Maxentius in 312 CE. Before the battle, he had a famous vision—he claimed to see a shining cross standing above the sun. Constantine's contemporary, the historian Eusebius, records that the cross had an inscription instructing the emperor that he would be victorious through this symbol. Eusebius writes that not only Constantine but also his whole army saw the miraculous sign, and later that night, the vision was further explained to Constantine in a dream. Constantine did march on to fight Maxentius in the Battle of Milvian Bridge under a standard in the shape of the cross, and his victory was decisive. This battle both marked Constantine's ascension to power over the entirety of the western part of the Roman Empire and his turn toward favoring the Christian religion—a change that would greatly affect an empire where Christians had previously been persecuted. Constantine's decision would pave the way for the official Christianity of the later Roman Empire, a unification of church and state that would change history. Constantine himself, however, never quite seemed to give up the old religion that had been his upbringing, and scholars have long debated the authenticity of his conversion.

Twelve years after his victory over Maxentius, Constantine acquired the eastern half of the empire as well. In 330, he renamed the city of Byzantium after himself, Constantinople, and declared it the new capital of the Roman Empire. This significant event is the reason historians label the year 330 as the beginning of the Byzantine Empire.

On Constantine's death in 337, his three surviving sons, Constantius II, Constans, and Constantine II, stepped up to inherit the rule of the empire. Before long, Constantine II was killed in a battle with Constans, and Constans himself soon died fighting a powerful leader, Magnentius, who rose up to challenge the throne in the west. Constantius marched from the eastern part of the empire to avenge his brother and defeat Magnentius. Consolidating his control of the Roman Empire, he pushed religious reforms farther than his father Constantine had; Constantius closed ancient temples and outlawed pagan rites. Needing help to orchestrate his rule of such a vast empire, he appointed his nephew Julian as Caesar. Upon returning to the capital of Constantinople, Constantius soon had to deal with a Persian invasion. He called for Julian to send troops from the west. But Julian and his armies took this request poorly, and Julian's men declared him Augustus, rival to his uncle. Julian's armies marched toward Constantinople not to help Constantius, but to conquer him.

On their way there, however, news came that Constantius had already become ill and died. He forgave Julian on his deathbed, leaving the younger emperor as his heir. Twenty-nine-year-old Julian, unbeknownst to his uncle, rejected the Christian religion that Constantine and Constantius had promoted. Julian's interests were instead in Hellenic culture and philosophy, and he chose to champion the ancient cult of the sun god. He reversed the religious laws made by Constantius, re-opening temples and doing his best to revive the old religion. While his attempts found some support, on the whole, they were met with ambivalence. Julian hoped that a decisive victory against the Persians would demonstrate the validity of his cause, and so in 363, he marched his armies against the Persians. Unfortunately for Julian's ambitions, his campaign was overwhelmed by the power of the Persian city he first approached. Turning toward a secondary target and harassed by Persian attacks, Julian's armies began to weaken. Julian himself received an injury that resulted in his death.

The young emperor's death left his army scrambling to put another ruler on the throne. After two unsuccessful attempts, they settled on Valentinian, a guardsman and a Christian. Valentinian named his brother Valens as his successor. Valens would rule in the east while Valentinian returned to the west. The brothers worked together to try to reduce corruption in the empire. Valens, in the eastern part of the empire, succeeded in suppressing a revolt and fighting against the Goths and Persians, though he eventually died in a battle against the Goths. Valentinian perished just shortly before Valens; Gratian, Valentinian's son, was left to try to hold the empire together. The west continued to weaken, while the east resumed the fight against the Goths. In the face of these difficulties, Gratian appointed an experienced general, Theodosius, to take command of the eastern part of the empire.

Theodosius, a Spaniard rising to power at age 33, did his best to fight off the Goths. However, the armies in the east were depleted, and he had to ask for Gratian's help. Still desperate for more men, Theodosius began to enlist a large Germanic contingent in his armies. In 380, not long after his ascension, Theodosius faced the additional challenge of a deathly illness. Expecting death, he called a priest and received baptism. But Theodosius did not die; instead, he became the first emperor to not only permit but fully embrace Christianity during his reign. As a result, in 391 he made the landmark proclamation that Christianity would now be the Roman Empire's sole religion. Not long after Theodosius' recovery, he and Gratian were able to come to an agreement to end fighting with the Goths. This treaty allowed Gothic peoples to settle peacefully inside the borders of the empire.

As wars ended and the economy improved, things were beginning to look more positive for the empire. But when Gratian was killed in an uprising, the political situation in the west became chaotic once more. Theodosius, at last, marched westward to put a rightful ruler on the throne. Unfortunately, in 395, as he was about to return to the eastern part of the realm, Theodosius died. The empire still hung together, but barely. The division Theodosius had drawn between east and west during his rule would become permanent, further emphasized by its alignment with the division between Latin and Greek-speaking territories. The east, unified by a developing culture centered around the Greek language, the growth of Christianity, and its independent government and economy, would continue in strength even as the west weakened.

Chapter Two

The Fall of the West

"A dreadful rumor has come from the West. . . . The city which had taken the whole world was itself taken."

—Saint Jerome

Theodosius had brought a tenuous peace to the empire, but his efforts were not destined to last long. The next few of his successors, starting with his sons Honorius in the west and Arcadius in the east, were weak emperors, controlled by the now powerful Germanic element in the military and government. Honorius' advisor, the real power behind the throne, was a half-German general named Stilicho. Stilicho defended the empire on several fronts, but his attempt to confront the raiding Huns and the Visigoths under Alaric in the east brought him into conflict with the advisors controlling Arcadius' eastern realm. Stilicho sent his troops to Constantinople, as Arcadius' advisors requested, but he put them under the control of the Visigoth General Gainas. Gainas succeeding in killing off Arcadius' advisors and taking control of the government of Constantinople, wielding his power behind the facade of the puppet emperor.

However, Gainas and many of his Visigoth troops were Arians, believers in a doctrine that had been ruled to be heresy at the First Council of Nicaea in 325. When Gainas tried to open an Arian church in Constantinople, the people of the city rebelled. They called upon another Visigoth, Fravitta, who was not a Christian at all, to drive Gainas out of the city. Arcadius, now free of Gainas, was still incapable of taking power himself. A small group of government officials seized control of the emperor and the empire. They escaped the threat of the marauding Visigoths under Alaric by sending them toward Italy and the western part of the empire. Perhaps they did not expect the extent of Alaric's success in the west—in 410, the Visigoths conquered and sacked the city of Rome.

Arcadius, on his death, was replaced by his son Theodosius II, who was only seven years old. Arcadius' last advisor, Anthemius, took the reins of power for the young emperor, sending troops to help the west hold the new capital at Ravenna against the Visigoths. He also worked to strengthen the walls of Constantinople. With Anthemius' death in 414, he left power over the young ruler in the hands of Theodosius' sister Pulcheria. Under Pulcheria and the Germanic military leaders who worked with her, the eastern empire was able to stave off the threat of the Huns for a time through bribes.

This period also marked the compilation of the *Theodosian Code*, a task that took nine years and was the first attempt at a complete compilation of Roman laws. When Theodosius II fell from his horse and died in 450, Pulcheria married a military official, Marcian, and put him on the throne as emperor. Within seven years, Pulcheria and Marcian had both died as well, leaving no heir. Their general, Aspar, did not take the title of emperor but did hold control of the east. The west, in a similar situation, continued to weaken.

Aspar knew that, due to his Arian beliefs, taking the throne of the Eastern Empire himself would lead to unrest and instability. He needed to install a puppet emperor to let him rule securely, and so he appointed a lieutenant named Leo. Leo seemed unlikely to contest Aspar's immense power as a military leader, and he had no heirs to present problems later. But Aspar seriously underestimated Leo. The new emperor began a subtle campaign to consolidate power for himself. Knowing that Aspar's power came from his position as head of the military, Leo looked for a way to diminish Aspar's military might. He found a solution through recruiting Isaurian soldiers, men from southeast Anatolia. One of the Isaurian leaders, Zeno, brought Leo convincing proof that Aspar's son was involved in a treasonous plot with the Persians. On this evidence, Leo could reward Zeno by making him both his son-in-law and equal in military rank to Aspar, thus chipping away at Aspar's power.

Beginning to take control of the government and army, Leo decided to send his forces to northwestern Africa in an attempt to help the struggling western part of the empire reclaim territory. Despite the massive army Leo raised, his chosen commander, his brother-in-law Basiliscus, led their troops to a sound defeat. This failure, conveniently for Leo, reflected poorly on Aspar as the head of the military. Aspar made one final, desperate bid to regain power, forcing Leo to have his younger daughter marry Aspar's son so that his son could be Caesar. This move angered the people of Constantinople so much that it gave Leo reason to promote Zeno to sole military commander and to quietly have Aspar assassinated in 471. Leo had at last gained control of the eastern empire, but just a few years later, in 474, he died. His son, Leo II, was only seven. Leo II also died within a year, and Zeno, his regent, was left as his successor.

Zeno, with his Isaurian heritage, was not popular. Leo's widow, Verina (who was also Zeno's mother-in-law), immediately began plotting against him; her brother, Basiliscus, joined her. They easily convinced Zeno that the city was rising against him and he needed to flee, and then they installed Basiliscus as emperor. Basiliscus soon bungled his reign by trying to dictate doctrine to the church, losing him the people's favor. He massacred Isaurians in the army, but then he placed an Isaurian commander, Illus, at the head of the troops he sent to deal with Zeno. Illus brought Zeno and his men back to Constantinople, where they deposed Basiliscus and placed Zeno as emperor once again.

In 476, while Zeno and Illus were busy re-taking control of Constantinople, the last emperor of the west was deposed in Ravenna. The Western Roman Empire had fallen, but the east still fought to survive. Zeno, trying to defend his territories from the Ostrogoths under Theoderic, used the fall of the west to his advantage. He convinced Theoderic to go take control of Italy; Theoderic's new campaign to set up a kingdom in Italy (which was successful) saved the Eastern Empire, and particularly the Balkans, from continued battling with the Ostrogoths.

Though Zeno died in 491, both he and Leo I had succeeded in strengthening the Eastern Empire dramatically. Zeno's successor, Anastasius, the husband of Leo's daughter, would continue this trend. Anastasius was unpopular with many in Constantinople, and yet his unusual interest in economics provided him with some profitable ideas. He cared about the administrative system and the bureaucracy and made it his goal to weed out corruption. One of his methods was to switch the government away from making payments through goods and towards the consistent use of cash, which could be more easily accounted for. He necessarily also stabilized the smaller coinage of the empire, switching the coins from a copper alloy to a pure copper coin. These measures, among others, served to bolster both the government and the army. Due to this, Anastasius succeeded in pushing back the Persians when they invaded in 502. When the emperor died in 518, he left a monumental sum in the treasury—enough to fund the empire's budget for three years. Anastasius, following on the work of his father Leo and the general-turned-emperor Zeno, left the Byzantine Empire as not only a stable state but also one quickly beginning to prosper.

Chapter Three

Rising to Glory

"Every man who is born in the light of day must sooner or later die; and how can an Emperor allow himself to become a fugitive? . . . As for me, I stand by the ancient saying: royalty makes the best shroud."

—Theodora, recorded by Procopius

Into the increasing peace and prosperity of the Byzantine Empire stepped an unlikely leader. Emperor Justin was almost 70 years old, came from a peasant family, and had little education. He had risen through the ranks of the army and was able to use his military support to take the throne. Justin's main advantage as a ruler was his nephew, Peter Sabbatius. Justin had adopted Peter and given him an excellent education, prompting Peter to change his name to Justinian in honor of his uncle. Justinian became his uncle's most important advisor. Together, one of their first moves was to heal the breach that had developed between the eastern and western churches.

Justinian also quickly proved that he was nobility unlike what the city was used to. Chariot racing was a hugely popular sport in Constantinople, with most people embracing the team of either the Greens or the Blues. Most family members of emperors took a neutral position, but Justinian did not hesitate to declare his support of the Blues. Being a fan of the Blues gave him connections to follow what was happening around the city. Through his affiliation with the Blues, Justinian met a young actress named Theodora and fell in love with her. At the time, being an actress was a scandalous profession, often considered synonymous with prostitution. There was even a law in place forbidding senators from marrying actresses. However, Justinian convinced his uncle to change this law so that he could marry Theodora. Soon after, Justin pronounced Justinian co-emperor, securing his nephew's right to the throne. Justin died in 527.

As Justinian stepped into his role as sole emperor, trouble with the Persians quickly drew his attention. The new emperor chose a man named Belisarius as his general—a significant choice, as Belisarius would become a leader whom Justinian relied on immensely. Justinian also began the task of collecting and updating the laws of the empire, going farther than Theodosius II had by trying to collect laws more comprehensively and also making new laws. The result was the *Codex Justinianus*, an important legal work that has provided the basis for many modern systems of law. Justinian elevated the chairman of his legal commission, John the Cappadocian, to the role of prefect of the east. John the Cappadocian was instrumental in making sure taxes were collected effectively; he particularly tried to make sure that the rich were proportionately taxed. This did not make him a popular member of Justinian's government.

Justinian, having earlier obtained a small victory in conquering the leaderless Crimea, decided to send a force under Belisarius against northwestern Africa. However, before he could take action on these plans, a riot began in Constantinople. The crowds of Greens and Blues at the Hippodrome—the chariot racing arena—began to shout, rallying together against the emperor and his taxes. The mob turned violent, with looting and fires breaking out throughout the center of the city. Justinian, Theodora, and the emperor's advisors took refuge in the palace. They contemplated escaping the city by ship. According to the historian Procopius, it was Theodora's counsel that convinced Justinian to stay in Constantinople. The riot finally ended when Belisarius, at the head of an army of mercenaries, conducted a massacre in the Hippodrome where 30,000 citizens were killed.

Through this horrific event, the Nika Revolt was ended, and power was firmly returned to the emperor's hands. Justinian used the burning of the city as a chance to rebuild Constantinople into a more splendid metropolis. The works Justinian commissioned included a lavishly decorated new senate house and a huge cistern to provide the city's water. But his most important project was the building of a new church, the Hagia Sophia. The old church, first built by Constantius II and then rebuilt by Theodosius II, had completely burned. Justinian commissioned his architects to design a building that would be unparalleled in the world. The church they constructed was not only huge, but also decorated with materials from around the Mediterranean—gold, marble, and precious stones arrived from places as far off as Egypt, Syria, and North Africa. The dome that formed the ceiling was the largest unsupported dome in the world, perched on layers of half-domes that spread its weight over 104 delicately-carved interior columns and massive exterior walls. The walls sparkled with mosaics, and the church would house an impressive collection of relics.

Justinian's building projects were not his only plan for increasing the glory of Byzantines. He still wanted to expand the realm of the empire through conquest. He finally was able to send Belisarius to take northwestern Africa from the Vandals in 533, a formidable feat which the general nonetheless accomplished in less than a year. Justinian then looked toward Italy, which the Ostrogoths still ruled. Belisarius succeeded in taking Naples and Rome and continued to push his army northwards. Just then, conflict seemed about to erupt with the Persians, so Justinian worked to make peace with the Ostrogoths so he could call Belisarius back. Belisarius captured Ravenna and then left Italy for Syria, where he stopped the Persians.

Justinian's expansion of the empire was suddenly stopped in 541 by the arrival of the bubonic plague. The death toll was enormous. Historians of the time recorded that over half the population of Constantinople died, and modern estimates indicate that about a quarter of the empire's total population may have succumbed to the disease. Justinian became ill himself. With the emperor unable to rule, Theodora took control. She relieved Belisarius of his position when rumors reached her that the military wanted to make him emperor if Justinian died. She also negatively impacted the empire's stability by encouraging a controversial doctrine within the Church. With reduced men in the armies, Theodora was unable to defend the empire from the Ostrogoths in Italy, the Moors in Africa, or the Persians to the empire's east.

Justinian, recovering in 542, found his empire in a challenging situation. Even as the plague died away in 544, internal chaos continued as the realm was struck by famine. Justinian restored Belisarius to his post and worked to recapture Africa, as well as to make peace with the Persians. Theodora died in 548, and by this time, the empire was beginning to look stable once again. Starting in 550, Justinian spent several years focused westward, defeating the Ostrogoths in Italy and the Visigoths in Spain.

The plague returned in 558. It was less severe this time, but still revenues for the government dropped along with the population, and the campaigns in the west were halted again. The Huns invaded the weakened empire and approached Constantinople itself, but Justinian paid them to leave. In 565, the 83-year-old emperor died. Justinian had expanded his empire's borders, patronized magnificent contributions to the arts and architecture, and added to the wealth of the Byzantines. However, the devastation of the bubonic plague at least partially undermined much of what he had worked for. Byzantine cities shrank, their governments could not collect taxes, and though universities and libraries continued to preserve literary and scientific knowledge, the arts and education declined. Justinian's heirs would prove unable to stop this downward trend for over two centuries.

Chapter Four

An Age of War

"In view of the extraordinary vigor and enthusiasm of the Arabs, what really needs explaining is not why they defeated the Byzantines but how Byzantium survived at all."

—Warren Treadgold

The three emperors who ruled at the end of the sixth century had neither the resources nor the vision that Justinian, the emperor who brought about the Byzantine Empire's golden age, had possessed. Justin II, Justinian's son-in-law, was much more interested in saving money than in saving the territories that his father-in-law conquered. Italy began to slip into the hands of the Lombards, while the Visigoths invaded Spain. Instead of sending reinforcements to the western parts of the Byzantine Empire, Justin renewed the war with the Persians. Only when the Persians captured a major city, Dara, did Justin realize he might have made a mistake. He responded by attempting suicide.

Following Justin II, two military men held the throne. Tiberias, the first of these, spent much of his reign trying to win back Dara. Tiberias' general and son-in-law, Maurice, inherited both the throne and an empire with serious financial difficulties. While the Byzantine Empire was facing attack on multiple fronts, Maurice saw no alternative but to cut into his soldiers' wages. He was able to end the war with the Persians and make great progress in driving back the invading Huns and Slavs in the Balkans, but ultimately, his inability to fund his troops was Maurice's undoing. In 602, under a leader named Phocas, Maurice's armies in the Balkans rebelled. They marched to Constantinople, beheaded Maurice, and made Phocas the new emperor—the first emperor of the east who did not peacefully inherit the throne since Constantine.

Chaos filled the empire. While Phocas tried to make sure other claimants to the throne were dead, the Slavs invaded the Balkans once again and the Persians attacked, destroying Dara. Supporters of the Blues and Greens were fighting each other throughout the empire. The Byzantine territory in northwestern Africa was the only part of the empire that seemed stable and secure, and the governor, Heraclius, decided to conquer Egypt for himself. In 610, Heraclius sent his son, also named Heraclius, to capture Constantinople. The younger Heraclius took the city and executed Phocas, declaring himself emperor.

Heraclius spent ten years bringing order to the disorganized armies and government, cutting wages and the budget in an attempt to bring the empire back from the verge of bankruptcy. Measures that had resulted in his predecessor Maurice's death succeeded under Heraclius; everyone could now see just how dire the empire's situation was. As the Persians continued their attacks on the empire and pushed farther into Anatolia, Heraclius' need for money to support his military became more and more desperate. At last, he turned to the Church. He asked the Church's leader, the Patriarch Sergius, for funds and received a large amount of gold and silver plate. With this, Heraclius began to amass his army in the east. In 624 and 625, leaving the Patriarch in charge of Constantinople, Heraclius gained several victories against the Persians. As the decade progressed, the Persians became divided as they experienced treachery and rebellion in their ranks. The Huns and Slavs also began to fight each other. This was great news for the Byzantines; by 630, Heraclius was able to reclaim much of their lost territory, as well as regaining the relic of the True Cross, which the Persians has taken from Jerusalem. The fortunes of the Byzantine Empire appeared to be rising.

But a new threat lay on the horizon. Throughout the 620s, Muhammad had been turning the scattered Arab tribes into a unified Muslim army. After conquering the Persians, the Arab force arrived at Byzantine borders in 633. Heraclius brought the True Cross from Jerusalem to Constantinople for greater safety and prepared for another long, slow war like he had fought against the Persians. The Byzantines fought the Arab armies in Syria and Egypt, suffering defeats in both places. Aging and ill, the emperor died in 641. Despite his attempt to leave the throne to the son of his second wife, the army and the people of Constantinople made Heraclius' grandson the new emperor. Constans II made a temporary truce with the Arabs, worked to strengthen and stabilize the military and unwieldy bureaucracy, and kept Italy and Africa in the empire—not unimpressive feats for an emperor who took the throne as a young teenager in a time of war and unrest.

Unfortunately for the empire, the next few emperors were also teenagers who had to struggle to maintain power in an empire that seemed to be quickly falling apart. The Arabs continued their steady advance into Byzantine territory. In 674, the Arabs arrived at Constantinople itself. The Arab siege was broken only when the Byzantines used a top-secret invention called Greek Fire to attack the Arabs' ships. Though the composition of Greek Fire is unknown today, records describe its devastating effects—even water could not put out the flames of this intense fire, and the Arab fleet suffered serious damage. As a result of the battle, the Arab caliph and the Byzantine emperor made a temporary truce. But by the turn of the century, the fighting had begun again. Carthage, the capital of Byzantine North Africa, fell to the Arabs, and they invaded Spain soon after. Internally, rebellions and revolts weakened already feeble emperors. When the Arabs turned their massive army and navy toward Byzantium once again, the empire appeared to be on the brink of collapse.

Chapter Five

The Destruction of Icons

"By the most obvious of objective measures, the disasters of the seventh and eighth centuries greatly impoverished Byzantine culture. Unless every available indicator is misleading, fewer authors wrote, fewer teachers taught, fewer artists and artisans created, and fewer builders built."

—Warren Treadgold

At this perilous moment, a new emperor took power. Leo III was a Syrian and a military commander, and he had a plan to deal with the oncoming Arab invasion. He attacked the navy with Greek Fire, and by allying the Byzantines with the Bulgars, he was able to stave off the Arabs on land as well. An exceptionally cold winter worked in Leo's favor, and the Arab army outside Constantinople suffered. When the caliph sent reinforcements in the spring of 718, he made the mistake of manning his ships with sailors mainly from Egypt and Africa, places where Christianity was the primary religion. These Christian crews turned against the caliph and supported Emperor Leo. The Arabs left by summer, and Constantinople was saved.

However, much of the empire lay in shambles, and many of the highly religious Byzantines reasoned that they must have incurred the anger of God. Leo, searching for a cause for this supposed divine wrath, settled his attention on icons. Icons were images designed to aid in worship, but some thought that this had gone were too far—that people had begun to worship the images themselves. The proliferation of these religious images certainly contrasted the policies of the successful Muslims, who rejected all religious imagery. Leo began his iconoclast—image destroying—campaign with the demolition of a mosaic of Christ on a palace gate. The action set off a riot in the city, but Leo, convinced of his position, continued to escalate his attempts to eradicate icons. This crusade brought the emperor into direct conflict with the pope. Leo responded by denying the authority of the papacy in the east and confiscating papal holdings. At Leo's command, thousands of icons were destroyed across the remainder of the empire, though many were hidden from the emperor's wrath and survived. Though many Byzantines did not support iconoclasm, Leo's continued victories against the invading Arabs lent him security on the throne.

Leo's son Constantine V ascended to the throne in 741. Though initially hampered by a revolt, eventually he carried on the iconoclastic campaign his father had started. In the 760s, realizing that many individuals in religious orders opposed iconoclasm, Constantine began a widespread persecution of monks and nuns. Like his father, Constantine achieved some major victories in battle, succeeding in driving the Bulgars out of the Balkans and the Arabs from Asia Minor. However, the schism in the empire between the iconoclasts and those who supported the use of icons was deep. Beyond this, most Christians outside of the empire or on its fringes condemned iconoclasm. Many who had once believed in the divine appointment of the emperor as the world's Christian ruler began to question his spiritual authority, and the place of Constantinople in the greater world began to change.

One of iconoclasm's greatest enemies lived within the walls of the palace itself. Constantine's son, Leo IV, married a Greek woman who strongly supported the use of icons. Leo IV was less violent in his embrace of iconoclasm than his father and grandfather—he ended the persecution of monks and nuns and tried to bring peace to the religiously divided empire. But when icons were smuggled to Irene in the palace, Leo IV tried to limit his queen's influence and punish the officials who helped her champion icons. Soon after, he mysteriously died. Irene became the reigning regent for their young son Constantine VI in 780, and the revitalization of icon usage was her primary objective.

Irene worked hard to put the icon back in its revered place in the Eastern Church, but her religious victory came at the expense of the attention to the military and protection of the empire's borders. By the time her son reached his twenties, she had yet to hand over power to him. When her generals urged her to put Constantine VI on the throne, she had them executed and her son imprisoned. The outraged army and citizens of Constantinople revolted, freeing Constantine and arresting Irene. Unfortunately, Constantine made a poor showing as an emperor and soon lost the advantage of his people's favor. Irene, still scheming to regain power, had him captured and blinded in 797; Constantine died as a result.

With this, Irene made history by becoming the first Byzantine woman to rule in her own right. Still, few supported her. The Pope declared that since the throne of Rome was now empty, Charlemagne, King of the Franks, would be crowned as the new Augustus. Charlemagne, in fact, offered to marry Irene. While Irene may have considered this proposal, her people were shocked and offended by the Pope's actions and the presumption that a Frank—a barbarian—could be installed as the emperor of the Christian world. A group of nobles proclaimed a general, Nicephorus, as their emperor. Nicephorus immediately had Irene immured in a convent. He began to work on expanding the empire's borders until he was killed in battle in 809. Another military leader, Leo V, took the throne and renewed the program of iconoclasm. He too lasted only a little over a decade before being assassinated, and icons were once again venerated. Yet another short-lived emperor held the throne after Leo.

In 829, a young emperor named Theophilus became the Byzantine ruler. Theophilus, though an iconoclast, valued learning and justice; he was known for making unusual choices as emperor. He wanted to be involved in the lives of his subjects, and sometimes walked the streets of Constantinople in disguise to talk with merchants and shop owners. A fan of the Blues, he once even entered one of the chariot races himself. More than this, his reign began the renewal of Byzantine education and scholarship. The iconoclast debate sparked the interest of many scholars in discovering ancient writings as they strove to prove their side of the argument. Theophilus opened the University of Constantinople, funded teachers, and even opened new scriptoria for copying manuscripts. Early in his reign, he was victorious in his battles against the Arabs, but he suffered a major defeat in 838 due to the rebellion of a portion of his army. Managing to recover from this event, Theophilus increased the pay of his army, assuring that rebellions would be less frequent in the future. Despite this, the balance in the treasury was fairly high upon his death in 842. The Byzantine Empire, having suffered repeated heavy blows over the course of almost two centuries, was finally beginning to recover and grow in prosperity once again.

Chapter Six
The House of Macedon

"Byzantium was no longer the sprawling empire of antiquity, but what had emerged from the wreckage of the Arab conquests was a vastly smaller, compact state with considerably more defensible borders . . . Byzantium had clearly found its footing again, and in addition to a resurgence of power and prestige, the empire now entered a startling cultural renaissance."

—Lars Brownworth

Though the Byzantine Empire could never regain the place in the world it had once held, signs indicated that the time had come for the empire to rise again. The Arab caliphate was beginning to splinter and weaken as the Byzantine population and prosperity began to slowly recover from years of natural disasters, war, and internal conflict. In 842, the two-year-old Michael II stood next in line to the throne upon his father Theophilus' death. Michael's mother, Theodora, acted as a regent for him along with her advisor, a eunuch named Theoctistus. Theodora, a supporter of icons, effectively ended the long-standing religious debate by claiming that Theophilus had renounced iconoclasm on his deathbed. In 856, Michael took the throne for himself with the help of his uncle,

Bardas. Michael became known as "the Drunkard," and was largely content to let his uncle make the decisions that governed the empire. During the years that Theodora, Theoctistus, and then Bardas held power, the empire continued regaining its footing.

Michael's decision to invite an ambitious wrestler known as Basil "the Macedonian" (who was not truly Macedonian) into his inner circle proved disastrous for himself and Bardas, though surprisingly, not for the empire. In 867, Basil managed to have both Bardas and Michael assassinated so he could take the throne himself. With this treacherous move, Basil established a dynasty that would become known as the "House of Macedon" and would bring another golden age to the Byzantine Empire.

Few citizens, if any, mourned the ineffective Michael, and Basil's immediate success as a ruler secured his rise to the throne. Basil saw the potential of the recovering empire and aspired to capitalize on the situation. The empire was now smaller, making it more defensible, and still had a fairly strong army, so Basil put his initial energy into rebuilding the depleted navy. The emperor soon began to launch an offensive campaign against the weakening Arab caliphate. A series of victories left Byzantine borders and territories more secure. Basil also intended to restore the grandeur of Byzantium on the home front. In Constantinople, he poured money into new building projects, refurbishing aging churches, restoring the beauty of the palace, and constructing a splendid new church known as the Nea Ekklesia ("New

Church"). In addition, during Basil's rule the empire experienced a resurgence of interest in discovering classical knowledge.

Unfortunately for Basil, his son died, leaving one of Michael's sons as heir to the throne. Basil opposed this teenaged successor, Leo. He placed Leo under house arrest for several years. Soon after Leo's release, Basil died in a suspicious-looking hunting accident. Leo VI was not a military man and did not have great success in the battles he orchestrated, but he did leave a lasting mark on the empire through his revision of the laws. Leo's *Basilica* built on the *Codex Justinianus* and left the empire internally stronger.

Leo VI died in 911, but during the following century other emperors continued to strengthen and expand the empire. Under Emperor Nicephorus Phocas and his successor John Tzimiskes, the Byzantine Empire grew to contain most of Greece and Bulgaria, as well as Armenia and northern Syria. They moved the military from operating almost entirely defensively to also having an offensive purpose, a mark of Byzantium's rise in power in relation to its neighbors. They increased the size of the navy and cavalry, as well. Though still much smaller than its earlier expanse across the Mediterranean, the growing empire was much more stable.

The military and geographic expansion during this time were made possible by the empire's burgeoning economy. A new system of bureaucracy and taxation and new coins with a higher percentage of precious metals encouraged this economic growth. Trade increased as furs from Russia, spices from India, and silk from China all flowed through Constantinople, the city that was quickly becoming the trading center of the world.

Byzantine culture developed rapidly as well. Both Greek Christian and secular literature were rediscovered, many works (about half of which are lost today) being described by the Patriarch Photius in his notes entitled *Bibliotheca* ("Library"). Many scholars penned works of history during this period, and others even developed and studied the Greek language further, compiling several dictionaries. The influence of the Byzantines' culture was felt outside of their borders, particularly in the Principality of Russia—the Byzantine influence spread Christianity there, and translation of parts of the Bible spurred rapid development of the use of written language in Russian lands. When the House of Macedon ended with the death of Basil II in 1025, the Byzantine Empire had reached its apex.

Chapter Seven
The Comnenian Revival

"Time, in its irresistible and ceaseless flow carries along on its flood all created things, and drowns them in the depths of obscurity. . . . But the tale of history forms a very strong bulwark against the stream of time, and to some extent checks its irresistible flow."

—Anna Comnena, opening to the *Alexiad*

New enemies would soon test the flourishing empire. The Normans began to attack Byzantine holdings in southern Italy, while in the 1060s, the Seljuk Turks made their first invasion into Byzantine territory in Armenia. Meanwhile, a series of mainly incompetent emperors did lasting harm to the empire's political and financial situation. By the end of the eleventh century, the army was depleted and the empire's coinage was devalued. Around half the territory of the empire had been lost to the raiding Turks and Normans. Though the cultural development of the Byzantines continued, the military disasters meant that survival of the empire once again appeared to be in question.

Into this bleak situation stepped a young man named Alexius Comnenus, already a renowned military commander despite his age. He was crowned emperor in

1081. He immediately was forced to turn his attention toward the Normans, who were poised to march toward Constantinople itself. Alexius' army was composed largely of mercenaries, and at the height of the important Battle at Dyrrhachium (in present-day Albania), these mercenaries betrayed the emperor. Alexius was injured, and the battle was lost. Guiscard, leader of the Normans, proceeded to conquer most of Greece while Alexius tried to rebuild his army. Alexius realized he would be unable to stop the Normans and appealed to the Hungarians and the Venetians with offers of gold and profitable trade agreements in exchange for an alliance. With the help of these allies, the Normans were beaten back. Guiscard, with his ambitions to take Constantinople, died in 1085, and the Norman threat was alleviated.

On the other side of the empire, the Seljuk Turks had continued their invasion, capturing Antioch in 1085 and Jerusalem in 1087. From here, their attacks turned to the coast of Asia Minor, taking several Greek islands as well as the harbor city of Ephesus (near modern Selçuk). But when the sultan of the Turks died, their weakened situation opened a window of opportunity to stop the invasion. Alexius still lacked military might himself, but he turned to Pope Urban II, as a fellow Christian, for help.

In response, Pope Urban launched the First Crusade. Knights from across Europe volunteered to go to the aid of the east in return for having their sins absolved. This was not what Alexius had in mind, as the knights about to descend on the Byzantine Empire were not under his control and it seemed entirely possible that many of them were just as interested in capturing Constantinople as Jerusalem. The "People's Crusade," a ragtag group of peasants under Peter the Hermit, was the first to arrive in Byzantium. This unofficial and unruly force terrorized the countryside on their way there, killing thousands of Jews as they looted and burned. Crossing into Asia Minor, the Crusaders pillaged Greek Christians until a decisive battle with the Turks destroyed the impromptu army.

The real Crusaders, European knights and their organized armies, arrived at Byzantium later. Alexius managed to convince almost all the knights to take oaths of allegiance to him, hoping for some security from the threat of the European forces. The Crusaders marched across Asia Minor and continued to Jerusalem, capturing the city and slaughtering its citizens regardless of their faith. But their relationship with Emperor Alexius, always strained, completely gave way and they returned none of their conquests to the empire. Luckily, while the Crusaders fought the Turks in Syria and Palestine, Alexius had been able to retake much of Asia Minor.

The mistrust between the Crusaders and the Byzantines continued to grow, and in 1107, Bohemund, a leader of the Crusaders and the son of the Norman Guiscard, landed a fleet near Dyrrhachium in an attempt to invade Byzantium. Alexius, now older and more experienced, surrounded Bohemund's army and won without a battle. Though indecisive border skirmishes with the Turks continued, the Norman threat was gone for the time being, and Alexius' death in 1118 left the empire on fairly stable footing once more. His daughter,

Anna Comnena, would contribute to the scholarship of the Byzantine Empire by writing the *Alexiad*, a history of Alexius' life.

Despite the relative success of Alexius' reign, the Byzantine army was still weak, the Turks still presented a threat, and the breach between the Byzantines and the Crusaders was deep. Alexius was followed by four successors, the other emperors who made up the Comnenus dynasty. John, his son and immediate heir, made little progress taking back territory from the Turks, and was hampered by plots against him by his own family members and unrealistic plans. John's youngest son Manuel followed him as emperor. Manuel warred with the Normans in Italy, the Hungarians, and finally the Turks, all with little long-lasting success. His death in 1180 left his ten-year-old son Alexius II as emperor, with Manuel's Norman wife Maria of Antioch as the real power behind the throne.

Without the appearance of a firm and proficient emperor on the throne, the empire began to totter. The Turks made their way into Asia Minor again, Hungary took back the border territories it had lost, and the Serbs declared their independence. Andronicus Comnenus, young Alexius II's cousin, marched an army to Constantinople and garnered the support of the people, who had never embraced the Norman Maria. Through a riot, Andronicus seized control, banished Maria to a convent, and soon was able to declare himself co-emperor with Alexius II. Before long, he murdered Alexius II. Andronicus spent much of his reign putting down rebellions and was known for his violent use of force, earning himself the epithet "the Terrible." He was overthrown in 1185.

Despite the unrest of the empire under the Comnenus dynasty, the wealth of the empire increased, partially due to population growth. The city of Constantinople grew to around 400,000 people, and in the countryside, farmers managed to produce enough food to feed themselves and the expanding cities and even to export. Industries such as weaving, pottery, brick making, and glass and metalwork continued to develop as well. Trade still brought in immense revenue for the empire.

Culturally, the rule of the Comnenians is often compared the Renaissance in Italy. The years 1081 to 1185 nurtured an interest in philosophy within Byzantium, and writers began to engage with ancient Greek classics and to develop works of poetry themselves. The art and architecture of the empire, in particular, flourished. Churches and monasteries displayed the work of artists in rich mosaics and illuminated manuscripts. Even the Normans wanted Byzantine artists to ornament their own most lavish churches.

But despite these cultural heights, the framework of the empire was failing. The Comnenian emperors had paid too little attention to the Turks and the European Crusaders, seemingly assuming their ancient empire to be superior. The weakness of the empire was becoming evident, and this time, its fall would be fatal.

Chapter Eight

The Final Decline

"They said that on the 29th of May, the third day of Saint Theodosia, at the third hour of the morning, the Hagarenes, that is the troops of Mehmet Celebi, entered the city of Constantinople. They also said that they killed the emperor. . . . Indeed nothing worse than this has ever happened or ever will happen."

—Fifteenth-century manuscript annotation

The two emperors who took the throne after Alexius II, Isaac Angelus and then his older brother Alexius III, suffered at the hands of both the Bulgarians and Turks. Additionally, revolts and rebellions sprung up across the empire as military commanders and governments officials tried to create their own independent realms. In the midst of a revolt in Constantinople in 1200, Isaac's son Alexius escaped the city and traveled to Germany to beg help from King Philip, who was Isaac's brother-in-law. Isaac had been deposed by his brother, Alexius III, and the former emperor was now blinded and imprisoned. Young Alexius, Isaac's son, allied himself with the Crusaders and the Venetians in hopes of putting his father back on the throne.

Emperor Alexius III was unprepared to face the powerful Venetian navy. He fled the city, leaving Isaac and Alexius (who now became Alexius IV) to take the throne back as co-emperors. Unfortunately, Alexius IV had promised a vast sum to the Crusaders in return for their assistance—a sum so great that he was now unable to pay it, especially since a large portion of the treasury had disappeared with Alexius III. His attempts to raise the money from the people of Constantinople not only made him unpopular but also did not succeed in raising nearly enough funds. In 1204 the young emperor was overthrown and executed, and his ailing father, Isaac, died as well, perhaps from natural causes.

The new emperor, Alexius V, stopped payments to his allies, the Crusaders and Venetians. As a result, the Venetian navy and Crusaders' armies attacked Constantinople. The city fell, and the Crusaders sacked, pillaged, and burned the town, destroying ancient churches, artwork, and monasteries. The emperor escaped, but the empire now lay splintered between rebel governors and pieces still held by the emperor. The central government in Constantinople, which had held the Byzantine Empire together for nearly a thousand years, was demolished.

Despite the crushing blow of the Fourth Crusade, somehow the empire managed to hang on to life for another two and a half centuries. The Crusaders put their own emperor on the throne, Baldwin of Flanders. Baldwin became known to the Byzantines as "the Latin emperor." The empire quickly succumbed to chaos. The Europeans pursued Alexius III and Alexius V, and Alexius III turned against Alexius V. A Byzantine potential claimant to the throne, Boniface, was given a small kingdom in northern Greece, but then invaded Thessalonica, where Alexius III ruled. Baldwin and the Latin forces were busy fighting Byzantines in Anatolia when the Bulgarians invaded them. This diversion allowed Theodore Lascaris, leader of the Byzantine rebellion in Anatolia, to proclaim himself emperor. He seated his throne at Nicaea. Theodore's claim was strong enough that the Patriarch crowned him as emperor in 1208. Still, this provided no end to the political chaos as other rulers claimed and fought over different pieces of the former empire.

Theodore's Empire of Nicaea provided a place of refuge for Byzantines. They carried Byzantine culture and Eastern Christianity there, and as the Bulgarians weakened the Latin forces, the Byzantines began to take back territory near Constantinople. The Byzantines at Nicaea were finally freed to attempt to recapture Constantinople when the Mongols unexpectedly attacked the Turks in 1242. The Crusaders' rule in Constantinople, now headed by Baldwin II, grew weaker and weaker. After Michael Palaeologus took the throne of the Empire of Nicaea in 1259, he began his attempts to reconquer Constantinople. He allied himself with the Genoese, a mighty power on the sea, to counterbalance the threat of the Venetian navy. Then, in 1261 he learned that the entire Latin garrison was gone, attacking an island elsewhere. The forces from Nicaea took the

Constantinople easily, and Michael arrived in the city shortly after to be crowned as Michael VIII.

Michael quickly set to work restoring the city of Constantinople to a semblance of its former glory. He even commissioned a new flag with an eagle on it—a reminder of the Byzantine Empire's roots in ancient Rome. Moreover, Michael began to make headway in the fight against both the Bulgarians and the Turks. Then a new threat arrived in the form of the Sicilians, led by Charles of Anjou, who wanted to put Baldwin II back on the throne. Michael escaped war for a time through diplomacy but eventually was forced to seek the help of Pope Gregory X in exchange for submission to the Western Church. The Byzantines understandably reacted negatively to this agreement, and Michael's hold on his empire was seriously weakened. Surrounded by enemies, the emperor had to keep fighting on multiple fronts even with the Sicilians held at bay.

In 1281, the new Pope who replaced Gregory X declared that Michael was excommunicated because his people had failed to submit themselves to the Western Church. Now Michael no longer had the protection of the Church, and the Sicilians and Venetians joined together to invade. Still, Michael stayed one step ahead of his enemies. He helped to spark and support a rebellion in Sicily, distracting Charles and ultimately costing the antagonistic king around half of his kingdom. Michael died soon after, but he had succeeded in restoring the Byzantine Empire to Constantinople despite huge obstacles and in the face of many enemies.

Though the dynasty Michael founded continued to hold the throne for almost two more centuries, few of his successors led with the same skill and daring that he had shown. But even as the strength of the empire declined, its culture still flourished and grew. Though many manuscripts had been lost in the fires of the Fourth Crusade, progress in science and medicine, art, architecture, and literature somehow continued. Michael VIII reopened schools such as the school of philosophy in Constantinople. In the fourteenth century, the Church of the Chora was decorated with its impressive frescoes and detailed mosaics that remain today. Scholars began to travel from Byzantium to Italy, transporting their knowledge of the Greek language and ancient Greek literature. Artists traveled to Serbia, Russia, and Bulgaria. Despite a civil war and the increasing troubles of the empire, high-quality scholarship continued until the late fourteenth century, when the bubonic plague returned, and war with the Ottomans began to take its toll.

The Ottomans began establishing themselves in Europe in the mid-fourteenth century and took the Balkans after the Battle of Kosovo in 1389. Within a few years, the remains of the Byzantine Empire were entirely surrounded. But Constantinople, with its defensible position and massive walls, was not easily taken. It continued to hang on through a siege in 1394, assisted by the Venetians and the Genoese. Other European countries, though claiming a willingness to help, did nothing. In 1402, the Mongols, led by Timur the Lame, attacked the Ottomans and captured Bayezid, the sultan.

Ottoman organization disintegrated as Bayezid's eldest son, Suleiman, attempted to consolidate power, giving Byzantium a short reprieve in the Ottoman war. As the Ottomans fought a decade-long civil war, the Byzantines and the European forces missed the opportunity to form an alliance that could drive the Ottomans out of Europe.

In 1437, the Byzantine Emperor John VIII traveled to Italy to meet with the Pope and arrange for Byzantium to be brought back into the Western Church. These negotiations were completed in 1440 in the Union of Florence, and the Pope began to make arrangements for another Crusade. The Crusaders, however, advancing against the Turks in the Balkans in 1444, failed. Another attempt in 1448 also failed. Time was running out for the Byzantines. In 1451, Mehmed II became the Ottoman sultan, and he immediately began plans to capture Constantinople. He started his siege in 1453. The sultan eventually took the city's harbor, despite the huge chain that blocked all sea traffic, by attacking the Genoese colony on the harbor's other side. With his new and powerful cannons, Mehmed was able to break through the strong walls of the city after two long months, on May 29, 1453. As the Ottoman troops sacked the city, the remaining citizens of Constantinople took refuge in the Hagia Sophia. When the Ottomans battered their way through the doors, they massacred everyone in the church.

The few Byzantine citizens who survived the Ottoman conquest of the city were sold into slavery, as around them Byzantine churches were converted to mosques and mosaics and frescoes were painted over. Though the Ottomans searched for the body of the last emperor, named Constantine just as the first emperor had been, they never identified it. With Constantinople defeated and its people killed and scattered, the Byzantine Empire was at last truly extinguished.

Conclusion

The last Byzantine emperor's two brothers held out in small territories outside the city for a few more years, until 1461. Then, at last, they too succumbed to the powerful Ottoman Empire. Still, the Byzantine fate had a resounding impact on the rest of Europe. Not only had the Byzantine Empire stopped the Ottoman advance for long enough to let Western Europe reach an advanced point of development, but also, the refugees who escaped the fall of Constantinople brought valuable knowledge and learning with them. They carried great classical works like the *Iliad* and the writings of Plato, which had been lost in the west but survived in Byzantium. Byzantine scholars became teachers to men like Petrarch and Boccaccio. In Italy, this resurgence of classical knowledge contributed to the beginning of the Renaissance.

The legacy of the Byzantines was not confined to Western Europe. Byzantine refugees traveled to Russia as well, leaving a strong heritage that became part of Russian culture. The imperial structure of the conquering Ottoman Empire borrowed heavily from Byzantine traditions. And even today, the Eastern Orthodox Church carries on the legacy of Byzantium across Eastern Europe. The light of Byzantine culture shone brightly, and their history, with its contributions to our modern world, is certainly worth remembering.

Printed in Great Britain
by Amazon